Once upon a time there was a Little Red Hen.
She lived on a farm with a cat and a rat and
a goat.

One day the Little Red Hen found some
grains of wheat.

She went to ask the other animals on the farm to
help her.

'Who will help me to plant the grains of wheat?'
she said.

But the cat and the rat and the goat said,

So the Little Red Hen planted the grains of
wheat all by herself.

She watched the wheat grow taller and taller.

Soon the wheat was ready to be cut.

The Little Red Hen went to ask the other
animals to help her.

'Who will help me to cut the wheat?' she said.

But the cat and the rat and the goat said,

5

So the Little Red Hen cut the wheat all by herself.

Then the wheat was ready to be taken to the mill to be made into flour.

The Little Red Hen went to ask the other animals to help her.

'Who will help me to take the wheat to the mill?' she said.

But the cat and the rat and the goat said,

7

So the Little Red Hen took the wheat to the
mill all by herself.

At the mill the miller ground the wheat into
flour.

Now the flour was ready to be made into bread.

The Little Red Hen went to ask the other
animals to help her.

'Who will help me to make the bread?' she said.

But the cat and the rat and the goat said,

So the Little Red Hen made the bread all by herself.

Soon the bread was ready to eat.

The Little Red Hen said to the cat and the rat and the goat,

'Who will help me to eat the bread?'

And the cat and the rat and the goat said,

11

But the Little Red Hen said, 'No, no, no.
You did not help me to plant the
grains of wheat.
You did not help me to cut the wheat.
You did not help me to take the wheat to
the mill.
You did not help me to make the bread
so I shall eat it all by myself.'